TABLE TALKS
Christmas is Jesus' Birthday, Not Yours

SPECIAL THANKS TO
God who guides my steps
and to my wife and son
who put up with my missteps

PARENTING BOOKS

Parenting Essentials:
Ten Things Every Parent Should Do

Do you know what you should be doing as a Christian parent? Do you understand what essential characteristics must be modeled for your children and teens? These are the questions this family-defining book seeks to answer.

The Christ Centered Home:
Turning Your Kids into Christ-Centered Disciples

Long before God established the nation of Israel to be His chosen people, and long before He established the church to spread His glory, He established the family to be the primary means of making disciples. Is your family fulfilling that mandate?

Lessons on Parenting

The Bible is full of detailed stories involving parents. In these insightful and meaningful narratives, Moms and Dads are found making choices and decisions that impact their children and those around them. So what can parents today learn from those parents of old? What happens in our families when we apply, or fail to apply, the lessons taught through these Scriptural accounts?

MORE TABLE TALKS DEVOTIONALS

TABLE TALKS
What It Means to be A Christian

TABLE TALKS:
Discovering Who God Really Is

TABLE TALKS:
Making a Difference for Jesus

FORWARD

NOTE: This devotional is designed to start on DECEMBER 1ˢᵗ.

God designed discipleship to take place in the home.

Yet, a survey by *The Barna Group* found the following troubling truth. "The survey data indicate that parents generally rely upon their church to do all of the religious training their children will receive...According to the research, parents typically have no plan for the spiritual development of their children; do not consider it a priority, have little or no training in how to nurture a child's faith, have no related standards or goals that they are seeking to satisfy, and experience no accountability for their efforts."

The results of this are predictable. One report found that over 70% of teens who regularly attended a church youth group stopped attending church altogether by the time they were twenty. Meanwhile, another report found that 88% of children who grew up in evangelical homes left the church after graduating high school.

Every day our children are bombarded by the culture and its message, yet they are not daily receiving the truth and message of Christ. Leaving the church to do that a few scant hours a week does little to combat what is being absorbed into our children's souls.

Think of the forty plus hours a week our children are in school. What message are they getting? Think of the fifty-four hours of media intake a week the average 12-18 year-old absorbs. What message is the culture giving? Think of the time spent with peers and coaches and tutors. What message are they instilling?

All of that time adds up to over one hundred hours per week. How can 1-3 hours of church per week possibly counter that? It cannot. By the time our children are eighteen and leave the nest, they also leave the church. This should come as no surprise to us. Their bodies are only following where their hearts and minds already are. Secure in the hands of the culture.

This is not what God intended.

Discipleship was meant to start and end in the home. Long before God created the nation of Israel to spread His glory and long before God instituted the church to share the message of Christ, God ordained the family to be the primary means of discipleship.

God says in Deuteronomy 4:9, "*Be very careful never to forget what you have seen the Lord do for you. Do not let these things escape from your mind as long as you live! And be sure to pass them on to your children and grandchildren...That way, they will learn to fear me as long as they live, and they will be able to teach my laws to their children.*"

God's plan from the beginning has been incredibly simple. "Parents, you teach your children about Me as you walk through life together. Then, when your children grow up and leave the home, they will turn around and do the same for their children."

That is the purpose of this devotional. Let it be a tool to help daily disciple your children and pre-teens.

Each day, you will find a Bible passage to read along with a devotional thought. From there, you will engage your children with a series of questions. The first is simply designed to get them talking, the rest focus on the day's lesson.

At the end of each devotional, you will be provided suggested prayers as well as ideas for object lessons that can further instill Biblical truths into your children.

God has called you to the great task of discipleship.

It is not your pastor's job nor your children's Sunday school teacher or youth leader's job. No, it is yours. Grab hold of that responsibility and watch as the Lord does awesome things in and through your family!

Well, what are you waiting for? Let the adventure begin!

DAY 1

READ ABOUT IT: Matthew 2:1-12

Did you start your Christmas list early this year? Like in April?

If so, you are kind of like the Weggerman family. They have eleven kids all under the age of fifteen, and once Thanksgiving is over all any of the kids can talk about is gifts, gifts, and more gifts. The toys they want. The video games they want. The bikes they want. The socks and underwear they want. Well, maybe not those things.

Isn't it interesting how so many of us are like the Weggermans? We treat Christmas as if it were our birthday. Why is it that we are so anxious to receive gifts on a day that should have nothing do to with us? After all, Christmas is not our birthday. It is Jesus' birthday.

THINK ABOUT IT
What is on your Christmas list this year?

Since Christmas is Jesus' birthday, who is it that should be receiving gifts on that day?

As you read the Christmas story in the Bible today, what gifts did Jesus receive on His birthday?

What can you give to Jesus on His birthday?

PRAY ABOUT IT
- Thank God for sending Jesus that first Christmas
- Ask God to help you remember what Christmas is all about

WHAT ABOUT IT?
- Have the kids make birthday cards for Jesus, then place them in a prominent place, like on the fridge or mantle
- Consider planning ahead to buy (or make) a birthday cake so that, on Christmas day, you can sing happy birthday to Jesus and eat some cake. This is a great way to remind the family who Christmas should center on
- Perhaps your younger children will struggle with the last question. Talk to them about how Jesus wants us to give Him our praise and worship, our time and talents, and to show love to others

DAY 2

READ ABOUT IT: Luke 2:1-20

Three year old Tracey got the nickname "Me-Me" for good reason. Everything she saw, she grabbed. And once she grabbed it, all you would hear was "Me, me, me, me." You could be sure that when "Me-Me" saw something she liked, she wanted it to be all hers and no one else's.

I think most of us would like to believe that we have outgrown three year old behavior. Yet, when it comes to Christmastime, there are many kids (and adults) whose attitude says, "Me, me, me...I want, I want, I want." It is as though we think Christmas should center on what we want, when really Christmas should be all about Jesus.

THINK ABOUT IT
Do you sometimes get like Tracey? Why or why not?

In our Christmas story for today, who is the focus of everything that is happening?

List the people/things that are focusing on Christ

in the Christmas story:

What can help you focus more on Jesus and less on yourself this Christmas?

PRAY ABOUT IT
- Thank God for His Son, Jesus Christ
- Ask God to help you focus more on Jesus this Christmas and less on yourself

WHAT ABOUT IT?
- Print out, or display on this screen, some pictures of animals, then prepare to "test" your kids
- Show them the picture of one of the animals and tell them to stare at it for twenty seconds. When that time is up, have them close their eyes, then ask what they are thinking about while their eyes are shut
- Do the same with another animal
- Often, our thoughts revolve around what we were just focusing on. Use this to discuss how, when we focus on ourselves, our thoughts usually center on "Me-Me," but if we spend time focusing on Jesus, our thoughts will change as well and we will be less self-centered

DAY 3

READ ABOUT IT: Mark 3:1-6

On December 1st, ten year-old Kyle happily put up a "Christmas Countdown" calendar in his room. It was a green felt calendar with tiny pouches below the first twenty-five days of December. As each day passed, young Kyle moved a little snowman from pouch to pouch. Now, Kyle did *not* normally like to wake up early for school each morning. But now that it was Christmastime, each morning he would excitedly jump out of bed and move the snowman into the new day's pouch.

Maybe you have a similar calendar and are eagerly counting down the days until Christmas. But think about this? Are you just as excited to celebrate the fact that Jesus was born that first Christmas? After all, He was born that first Christmas so that He could make a way for you to have eternal life in Heaven!

THINK ABOUT IT
What kind of Christmas countdown does your family usually do?

How excited for Christmas are you?

How excited are you that Jesus came to die for your sins?

All of the Old Testament was written to point toward Jesus' coming, yet what happened in our Scripture when Jesus finally came?

Are you focused on the right things this Christmas?

PRAY ABOUT IT
- Thank Jesus for coming to die for your sins
- Ask God to excite you about what Jesus has done

WHAT ABOUT IT?
- On a sheet of blank paper, write out "Happy Birthday Jesus!" in big letters that fill the page
- On another sheet of blank paper, write out "Happy Birthday Jesus!" in smaller letters that are centered in the middle of the page. Surround those words with bright colors, images, and other distracting things. In

short, make it difficult for your children to focus on the message of the paper
- Stand about 12 to 15 feet from your kids and show them the first paper. Have them read the phrase, then do the same with the second sheet
- Discuss how it was much more difficult to focus on the message of the second paper because it was "drowned out" by everything else
- Go on to talk about how all the "extra-stuff" of Christmas causes us to miss the fact that it is really about Jesus' birthday, and your family needs to work hard to focus on that

DAY 4

READ ABOUT IT: Matthew 12:15-21

Delayed by a meeting at work, Shawn's father arrived late for his baseball game. Quickly running over to the dugout, Dad asked Shawn what the score was.

"We're losing 12-0." Shawn said, keeping his eye on the game.

"Yikes!" replied Dad, "I'll bet you're pretty upset, huh?"

"Why should I be upset?" answered the little boy. "We haven't even gotten up to bat yet!"

Hope is a great thing, isn't it? Shawn wasn't upset because he believed his team could score lots of runs when they got their chance to bat. That's a great attitude because, when you have hope, it seems like anything is possible!

THINK ABOUT IT
Have you ever felt hopeless? When was it?

Where does our Scripture say the hope of the world is found?

This Christmas, where are you looking for hope?

Who do you know that needs to hear about the hope that Jesus can give?

PRAY ABOUT IT
- Thank Jesus for being the hope of the world
- Ask God to use you to tell people who are feeling hopeless about the hope they can have in Christ

WHAT ABOUT IT?
- Fill a sack or backpack with heavy objects like rocks or weights. Fill a second, equal-sized, backpack or sack with very light objects like crumpled up paper
- Have your kids walk around the room a few times with the heavy backpack then have them do the same with the second one
- Discuss how it is no fun walking around carrying a heavy load
- Move on to talk about how hope "lightens our load." Jesus came to give us hope by taking

all the bad stuff in our lives, like sin, so that life is easier to deal with

DAY 5

READ ABOUT IT: Isaiah 7:14; Colossians 1:25-27

This is the time of the year when we start to see a lot of Santa Claus. He's all over TV commercials; he's starring in movies; he's at the mall, he's riding on fire trucks in parades; he's making guest appearances at Walmart; he may even show up at your school. And along with Santa, we also see a lot of Frosty, Rudolph, and all sorts of other Christmas characters. But where are all these folks the other eleven months of the year?

Then there is Jesus. He doesn't just show up at Christmastime. He is with us every day of the year and all the days of our lives.

THINK ABOUT IT
Why is Jesus way better than Santa?

The Bible says that Jesus' name is also Immanuel—which means "God with us." Why is it so important to remember that Jesus came that first Christmas so that He could be with you forever?
The Bible doesn't just say Jesus wants to be *with*

us. It also tells us what in Colossians 1:27?

How great is it to know that Jesus can live *in* you?

PRAY ABOUT IT
- Thank God for being with you and in you
- Ask God to remind you how much greater He is than Santa Claus

WHAT ABOUT IT?
- Get two shoe boxes or other, equal-sized, empty boxes. Fill one with goodies—like candy, coins, and/or small toys. Leave the other one empty
- Wrap both in Christmas wrapping paper (optional)
- Have the kids open up each box, making sure they open the empty one first
- After they have opened both boxes discuss how the empty box isn't nearly as good as the full box
- Likewise, without Jesus, our lives would be pretty empty. Yet, when Jesus fills us, life gets a whole lot better!

DAY 6

READ ABOUT IT: Mark 15:16-20

You've probably seen lots of Christmas pictures that have little baby Jesus snuggled in blankets lying in a cute manger. The stable He is sleeping in seems well lit and warm, and the hay appears bright yellow and clean. The hay even looks comfortable enough to sleep on. Meanwhile, the animals, all looking clean and happy themselves, surround Jesus. It just seems so wonderful!

However, that is *not* how it was at all. Jesus was not snuggled in blankets. He was wrapped in thin strips of cloth. The stable was not well-lit, but rather very dark and most likely a cave. The straw was cold and hard and dirty. The animals were messy and smelly. It certainly was no place for a baby to be born, let alone baby Jesus.

Think of it. Jesus was born in that dirty, stinky, cold, dark place for one reason—to save us from our sins.

THINK ABOUT IT
Can you think of pictures of Jesus in the manger? How does the scene usually look?

What does it mean to you that Jesus—God in the flesh—was willing to be born in a dirty, stinky place?

What does it mean to you that Jesus was willing to come that first Christmas so that He could grow up and die for your sins?

PRAY ABOUT IT
- Thank Jesus for what He was willing to do for you
- Ask God to focus you on Jesus, and not on gifts, this Christmas

WHAT ABOUT IT?
- If you live near a barn or stable that houses animals, schedule a trip to take your kids there, so they can better experience the smells and sights of a real barn
- You can also work to create the feel of the stable. If you have a room with hardwood floors, take the kids in there when it gets dark
- Have only a single candle lit. If you live in a cooler climate, open the window so it is cold in the room. Have some stinky items lying around like dirty socks, athletic shoes, bad

milk, etc. and have the kids take turns smelling these things
- While still in the room (or at the barn/stable), talk about the cold, dark, and smelly night that Joseph, Mary, and Jesus endured in that stable
- Discuss how much God loves us that He would become flesh and enter our world in such a way

DAY 7

READ ABOUT IT: Hebrews 2:14-18

Eight year-old Sam needed crutches to walk because one of his legs was deformed. Life could be pretty tough for him sometimes since he could not run and jump and play like all the other kids in his neighborhood. Sam also knew what it was like to get teased, laughed at, and bullied for being different.

So when Sam found out that his neighbor's dog just had puppies and one of them was crippled, he got really excited. He begged his parents to let him have that crippled puppy because he just knew that puppy would need someone who understood what it was like not to be able to run and jump and play like everyone else.

Sam's parents did let him get that puppy, and the two quickly became best friends. Did you know that, in a similar way, Jesus became like us so that He could show how much He understands us? Jesus took on flesh and blood to feel what we feel, do what we do, live like we live, and then die for our sins so we could be forgiven.

THINK ABOUT IT
If you could have any pet in the world, what kind of pet would you have? Why?

According to our verses for today, why did Jesus become flesh and blood?

How does it make you feel to know that God became like you, so that He could help you?

What can you do to help others this Christmas?

PRAY ABOUT IT
- Thank God for sending Jesus that first Christmas
- Ask God to use you to help others this Christmas

WHAT ABOUT IT?
- Ask your children if they have ever been sad, ever been teased, ever felt pain, ever been lonely, ever been betrayed by a friend, ever been scared, or ever been hit
- Talk about how the Bible says Jesus had times of sadness. He was teased. He felt

pain and was abused. He was lonely and scared. And He was betrayed by a close friend and badly hurt by people who beat Him and hung Him on a cross
- Discuss how Jesus went through all of that so we could know that we have someone who understands us. Jesus has been through what we've been through
- When we are struggling, we can come to Jesus in prayer, and He will give us the support and strength we need

DAY 8

READ ABOUT IT: John 3:16-18

Just a few weeks before Christmas, Melody found herself as a single mother. Her husband took all the money out of their bank account and just left. Now, Melody was alone at Christmas with three young children to take care of. Since they had no money, they could not even afford a Christmas tree. Instead, they painted one on the wall and glued bottle caps to the "branches" as makeshift ornaments.

Melody, with tears in her eyes, told her children they would not get any presents this year. She thought this would devastate the kids. But eight year-old Sarah just smiled and said, "It's alright mom. We have each other; we have love; and we have Jesus. That's enough for us!"

THINK ABOUT IT
How would you react if you heard you weren't getting any Christmas presents this year?

What was the purpose of Jesus' coming according to our verses for today?

Christmas is about God's love for us in sending Jesus. If Christmas did *not* include gifts, but was just about God's love and Jesus' coming, would you be okay with that? Why or why not?

PRAY ABOUT IT
- Thank God for His great love and His great Son, Jesus
- Ask God to help you focus more on Jesus this Christmas and less on gifts

WHAT ABOUT IT?
- Check out the Operation Christmas Child website
- It is too late to get involved in packing a shoe-box, as the collection week was in November, but talk to the kids about how your family can still support children around the world who would not have Christmas without the generosity of others
- You may consider packing shoe-boxes next year or donating to the cause and help ship those shoe-boxes around the world

DAY 9

READ ABOUT IT: Romans 5:15-17

Eleven year-old Stephen's dad was thinking back to some of the great Christmas presents that he received as a kid. One year, he got a video game system called *Intellivision*. He and Stephen's aunt Anne spent countless hours playing video games on that thing. He remembered another time when he got a Fender electric guitar and Peavey amplifier. Wow!

"But, you know," Stephen's dad started to say. "All of those things are long gone now. That's the problem with things. They never last. They get old. They break. They get boring, or they get lost. Yet, the gifts that Jesus brings never get old, never break, never rust, and never get boring. They just keep getting better and better as the years go by."

THINK ABOUT IT
What was the best Christmas present you ever got?

Looking at our Bible verses for today, what great "gifts" do we get from Jesus?

Why are these gifts much better than regular Christmas gifts?

Did you know that you could be a gift to people? In what ways do you think that you could bless people this Christmas?

PRAY ABOUT IT
- Thank Jesus for being the greatest Christmas gift of all
- Ask God to use you to be a blessing to others

WHAT ABOUT IT?
- Brainstorm ways you and your family can serve others this Christmas
- Some ideas to consider: Ask your pastor if there are needy families in the community, volunteer at a food bank, a soup kitchen, or homeless shelter
- Bake cookies or brownies as a family and take them to a nursing home or share them with your neighbors
- Give up a gift that you want this Christmas and donate the money that would have been spent to a Christian charity

DAY 10

READ ABOUT IT: John 14:12; Acts 9:32-43

Think of all that Jesus has done. He gave blind people sight. He healed people who could not walk. He cured the sick of their diseases. He drove demons from the possessed. And let's not forget that Jesus even raised the dead!

But that's not all. Jesus calmed storms. He turned water into wine. He multiplied a few loaves and fishes into a feast to feed thousands. And He even walked on water.

All of that is *amazing*! But do you know what is even more amazing? Jesus said that *we* would be able to do greater things than He did.

THINK ABOUT IT
What is something amazing that you have done?

What was Peter able to do because he had God's Spirit in his heart?

This Christmas, do you think Jesus could do

something amazing through you for someone who needs a miracle?

Who do you know that needs a miracle?

PRAY ABOUT IT
- Thank Jesus for all the amazing and wonderful things He has done
- Ask God to use you to make a difference in people's lives this Christmas

WHAT ABOUT IT?
- Create an obstacle course inside your home, but do not let your children see it
- Blindfold the kids and take them to the course. Have them try to navigate through the course blindfolded
- After it proves impossible, allow them to take off their blindfold and try again
- Discuss how it was much easier to navigate the course without the blindfold
- Move on to talk about how many people all around the world are struggling through life, like your children struggled through the obstacle course blindfolded. They need Jesus to do a miracle, so that life will become easier for them

- After talking this through, spend time in prayer for those you listed under the last question

DAY 11

READ ABOUT IT: Mark 1:29-34

Thirteen year-old Asha was burning with fever in a remote village far from any doctors or medicine. It seemed she did not have long to live. Several Christians in the village heard of Asha's situation and rushed to her bedside. They began praying, and suddenly the fever vanished and Asha got out of bed!

Eleven year-old Jashun severely injured his knee. It got badly infected and the infection destroyed all the nerves and muscles in his knee...and then started spreading. Doctors were about to amputate. Then Mary came to pray. One week later, Jashun's knee and leg were completely healed.

Many people think Jesus doesn't do miracles anymore, but you and I know that He does!

THINK ABOUT IT
What miracles did Jesus do in our Bible verses for today?

What miracles did Jesus do for Asha and Jashun?

Do you think Jesus can still do miracles today? Why or why not?

Do you think that He could use you to pray for a miracle?

PRAY ABOUT IT
- Thank God for the miracles He still does today
- Ask God to use you to pray and work for miracles to happen for people today

WHAT ABOUT IT?
- Pray again for the people you prayed for yesterday
- Pick a country in the world that is really struggling. Not sure which one to pick? Go to www.operationworld.org This great website will give you "prayer requests" for every country in the world
- Commit, as a family, to pray every day for the rest of this year that Jesus will do a miracle in that country

DAY 12

READ ABOUT IT: Luke 2:41-52

Eleven year-old Tami came home from school one day with an interesting story to tell. She said that her class was practicing for the school's "Winter Program" and one of the songs they were singing was "Go Tell it on the Mountain." Now, Tami knew this song well from all the times she had sung it in church.

However, Tami was confused because the school was using "new words." Instead of singing, "Go tell it on the mountain that Jesus Christ is born," the school had changed the words to "Go tell it on the mountain that *a little baby* is born."

At first, Tami's parents thought it was a joke, but it was true. Unfortunately, stuff like this isn't just happening in a couple places. It seems Jesus' name is being removed from *lots* of things and places.

THINK ABOUT IT
Do you sing Christmas songs about Jesus in your school?

Who did Mary and Joseph "lose" for three days?

It seems Jesus is being "lost" in our culture. It is harder and harder to find Him talked about or sung about. But what can you do to help make it easier for people to "find" Him?

PRAY ABOUT IT
- Thank Jesus for His willingness to come that first Christmas so that He could die for our sins
- Ask God to use you to help people find Him this Christmas

WHAT ABOUT IT?
- Play hide-n-seek with the kids, insisting that you are the one who gets to hide first
- Hide in a spot that is impossible for the kids to find you, but let your spouse or an older child know where you will be ahead of time
- After a while, let the spouse or older child guide the others to where you are
- After the kids find you, discuss how it is much more fun to play hide-n-seek when you can find the people you are seeking
- Move on to discuss with your kids how our culture is making it harder and harder for

people to find Jesus, but just as someone guided them to find you, so they need to help guide others to find Jesus

DAY 13

READ ABOUT IT: Isaiah 9:1-6

Have you ever had the perfect day? No one caused you any problems and you didn't cause anyone else problems? No one yelled or cursed or got hurt or was sad. Everyone just seemed happy and joyous and full of fun. Have you ever had a day like that?

Those kinds of days seem pretty rare, don't they? Even when we try as hard as we can to have the perfect day, someone or something comes along to ruin it all! Thankfully, one of the great messages of Christmas is that God came into an imperfect and messed up world to be with us. This is awesome news indeed because there aren't many perfect days out there, so we need God a lot!

THINK ABOUT IT
Have you ever had the perfect day? If so, what made it perfect?

Isaiah 9 is an Old Testament prophecy about Jesus coming. What bad things are listed in these verses that Jesus would be born into? (See verses 1 and 4)

What are some rough things going on in your life or in your family that Jesus can come into and change?

Who do you know who needs Jesus to come into their imperfect life?

PRAY ABOUT IT
- Thank God for sending Jesus that first Christmas to be with you through life
- Ask God to use you to bless others this Christmas

WHAT ABOUT IT?
- Set up a series of ten to twelve dominos. (If you do not have dominos, you can use *Lego* pieces, *Scrabble* tiles, or even hard cover books)
- Gather your kids around what you have set up and talk about how you carefully arranged these dominos (or what you used), just exactly as you want them to be. Yet, one thing can ruin it all
- Tip over the first domino and watch as they all fall over
- Discuss how life is like that. We want things to be just perfect and we work to make it

that way, but one little thing can ruin it just that quickly
- Set everything back up and, as you do, explain that this is what Jesus does. He takes our imperfect lives that are messed up and He helps make everything all right again
- And when things fall apart all over again, He is right there to help pick back up the pieces that time as well

DAY 14

READ ABOUT IT: Luke 1:26-38

Imagine if God came to you one evening and said, "I just want you to know how much I love you. And I am soooo proud of how you are living that I want to bless you in a super-awesome way!" I think if that happened you would be pretty excited!

However, what if after God said that, He also added this, "Oh, and after I bless you, your life is going to get incredibly hard. Friends will make fun of you. The person who you were going to marry you will not want to marry you anymore, and you're not going to be able to do anything about it."

If that happened, you would probably think, "Hey, I thought You just said You loved me. I thought I was going to be blessed. I didn't think that life would get harder after that!"

THINK ABOUT IT
This is the exact kind of situation Mary was in. God was going to bless her, but her life would become very difficult for a while. Yet, how did Mary respond to this in verse 38?

What kind of attitude do you usually have when life gets hard?

Do you think that life should always be easy if you are a Christian and love God?

Why do you think that God has us go through trials sometimes?

PRAY ABOUT IT
- Thank God for the lessons He teaches through tough times
- Ask God to help you have a good attitude in tough times

WHAT ABOUT IT?
- Have the kids lie on their backs and give them two pillows to "bench press" ten times
- After they do so, carefully lie across one child and tell him or her to bench press you ten times. (You can help by pushing yourself up as your child pushes but continue to make yourself "heavy" so that it is difficult)
- When finished, discuss how it is certainly much easier to bench press pillows. Then ask

your child if he thinks one can build strong muscles by lifting pillows
- When the answer comes back as "NO!," ask if he could build strong muscles if he lifted heavy things
- Go on to talk about how we don't grow strong by lifting easy things but by lifting hard things. Likewise, we don't grow strong in character by having all easy days. When things are hard, that is when God can help us grow the most

DAY 15

READ ABOUT IT: Matthew 1:18-25

Bobby was having the worst Christmas season ever. During Thanksgiving, his mom and dad fought almost non-stop. And it just got worse after that. Now, here it is, less than two weeks before Christmas, and Bobby's dad just packed up his stuff and left! Bobby could only sit in his room and cry. Christmas was supposed to be the most exciting and fun time of the year. Now it all seemed ruined.

Bobby is probably feeling a lot like Joseph did in our Bible story for today. Joseph was really excited about getting married and starting family, then boom! He hears the news that Mary already is going to have a baby! It couldn't have been any worse for Joseph.

THINK ABOUT IT

Can you think of a tough time that God saw you through? When was it?

How did God encourage Joseph during his tough time?

Like we saw yesterday, tough times can happen to anyone at any time. But how can trusting God help us through these times?

What can you do this Christmas to encourage someone who may be feeling down or going through a tough time of their own?

PRAY ABOUT IT
- Thank God for encouraging you in tough times
- Ask God to use you to be a blessing to others

WHAT ABOUT IT?
- There are many people who feel lonely and discouraged at Christmas— hospital patients, shut-ins, nursing home residents, and widows are just a few
- Have your family do something nice for some individuals in situations like those—make Christmas cards, bake cookies, brownies, *Rice Krispie* treats, or other tasty treats, and take them to those in nursing homes, to shut-ins, widowed neighbors, etc.
- Spend some time in prayer for people who feel lonely and discouraged during the holiday season

DAY 16

READ ABOUT IT: Luke 2:1-7

Michael's family lived in a rural area of Wisconsin on a large farm with two huge barns. One of the farm chores that Michael had was to help clean those barns, which he did *not* like to do. Dirty hay was scattered everywhere. Farm animal droppings, as well as mice and rat droppings, were also everywhere. Flies buzzed around all the animals and all the droppings then buzzed around him too. And on top of all that, it just plain stunk in there!

As we talked about on Day 6, Jesus was born in that type of place. Even though Christmas pictures make the stable look warm, clean, and cozy, it was not. It was dirty, stinky, and cold. Jesus was born in a messy place on a messy world, because He wants to make a great difference in our messy lives.

THINK ABOUT IT
What is the messiest place you have been? The smelliest?

Can you tell how much Jesus loves you because He was willing to be born in such a stinky and dirty place?

What are some "messy" areas in your life that Jesus can help you clean up?

Who do you know that is in some messy situations and needs you and your family to pray for them?

PRAY ABOUT IT
- Thank Jesus for coming into our mess so that we could be cleaned up by Him
- Pray for the people you listed under the last question

WHAT ABOUT IT?
- Play a few games of "Pick up the Trash" with the kids
- The game is quite simple to play. Divide a room in half and place 15 to 20 pieces of crumpled paper on both sides (make sure the amounts are equal)
- Have parents on one side and kids on the other. On the signal, both teams pick up the "trash" on their side and throw it to the other team's side. At the end of one minute, call time and count the pieces on each side

- The team with the *least* amount on their side wins
- After you have played a few rounds, talk about how the world is messy place filled with a lot of hurting people, but Jesus came to clean it up by bringing hope and healing
- Discuss how praying for, and helping, others is a way your family can partner with Jesus in the "clean-up process"

DAY 17

READ ABOUT IT: Hebrews 11:32-38

A couple days ago, we met Bobby, who was having the worst Christmas season ever. His father had packed up all his things and moved out. Bobby was devastated. He just stayed in his room and cried and prayed.

Bobby figured if he prayed enough, God would bring back his dad. However, he's been praying for three days and now Mom has told him that, not only is Dad not coming back for Christmas, Dad is not coming back at all!

"It's *not* fair!" Bobby cried to Mom. "I've been praying to God. He should bring Dad back."

Mom gave Bobby a big hug and a kiss. "Oh, Bobby," Mom started. "God never promised that everything would be easy or work out the way we want it to. He did promise, though, to be with us through it all."

THINK ABOUT IT
What were some tough things the people in our Bible verses were going through?

In our Bible verses, some things worked out great and some things worked out terribly. Why do you think bad things happen to good people sometimes?

How does knowing that God is with you during tough times help you get through those times?

PRAY ABOUT IT
- Thank God because He promises to never fail or leave you no matter how bad life can get
- Ask God to remind you that He is with you
- Ask God to use you to remind others that He is with them as well

WHAT ABOUT IT?
- Discuss how God can take terrible situations and use them to do great things
- If there are difficult things going on in your family now, (or you know of a family in the midst of difficulty), have a time of prayer asking God to work in awesome ways

DAY 18

READ ABOUT IT: John 14:18; John 16:33

Mr. and Mrs. Johnson have fostered almost thirty different children. Because they have had so many children in their home, the Johnson's have some great and funny stories to tell. They also have some sad stories.

One of the saddest involves a boy named Miller. Miller's mom had serious problems and his father was very unreliable. Because of this, Miller was put up for adoption. He had been in foster care for over five years and was starting to get very sad thinking he would never be adopted. But then it happened. A couple came along and adopted Miller. Even better, it was Christmas time, so it was like the best Christmas present he had ever gotten in his life.

It seemed like the perfect happy ending to what had been a long, sad story. However, just a few months later, the family decided they no longer wanted Miller and returned him to foster care. Amazingly, two years later, he was adopted again. But that family also decided to put him back in foster care.

THINK ABOUT IT
How would you feel if you were Miller?

Even though it may seem to Miller that no family wants him, what good news could you give him after reading John 14:18?

Why is it so important to know that Jesus came that first Christmas so that we never have to be alone?

PRAY ABOUT IT
- Thank Jesus for His willingness to come that first Christmas so that we don't ever have to be alone
- Ask God to use you to help people find Him this Christmas

WHAT ABOUT IT?
- You can share with your family that Miller's story is a true story, and he is now with a third family
- Discuss how God never fails or forsakes no matter how bad things may seem, and be sure to say a prayer that Miller has found a "forever family"

DAY 19

READ ABOUT IT: Romans 8:31-39

Sunday was a great day for Ella. She woke up early and had a prayer time before church. Later, she drove to church with her parents and went to both Sunday school and the Worship Service. After that, she helped her mom bake cookies and clean the kitchen. By the end of the day, Ella was feeling good and went to bed thanking God for a great day.

Monday, however, was not starting out as a great day. Ella began fighting with her sister, Emma, over who could use the bathroom first. Ella even used a bad word when yelling at Emma which got her in trouble with her parents. When it came time to pray before breakfast, Ella couldn't bring herself to do it. She thought, "How could God want to hear from someone sinning so much?"

THINK ABOUT IT
Do you think God only wants to talk to you when you are having a good day?

Do you think God only loves you when you are doing well, or does He love you all the time?

What do our Bible verses for today tell us about God's love?

How is Christmas really a sign of God's great love for us?

PRAY ABOUT IT
- Thank God for His love that never ends and is always there for you
- Ask God to remind you that He will always love you

WHAT ABOUT IT?
- Take one salt crystal and place it on the kitchen table
- Tell your family that the table represents God's love while the salt crystal represents our love
- Blow the crystal off the table and talk about how our love isn't so strong and steady
- Next, try to blow the table away
- Go on to discuss how God's love is strong and steady. It is always there and isn't going anywhere
- As an extra way to instill the lesson, you can place three or four salt crystals on the table

- Then say things like, "You're mean to me." "You broke a promise." "You just sinned big time." Each time you say one of the phrases, flick a crystal off the table
- When all the crystals are gone, say the same things again only this time flick the table each time
- Reinforce that our love may "disappear" when bad things happen, but God's love isn't going anywhere

DAY 20

READ ABOUT IT: Hosea 6:1-6

His parents called him "Roller Coaster Robert" because life with Robert was like one giant, never-ending roller coaster. One day, Robert would be kind and loving and nice to his parents and two sisters. But the next day, if someone said or did something he didn't like, he would be angry and mean to his sisters and disrespectful to his parents. It was indeed like being on a roller coaster. One day, Robert was climbing up higher and higher and the next day he came crashing down bringing everyone with him!

Unfortunately, all of us have some Robert in us. Instead of making choices based on what God wants or what is right, we sometimes make choices based on how we feel. When we feel good, we make good choices. But when we feel bad, we make bad ones. It's a roller coaster no one should be on.

THINK ABOUT IT
Are you sometimes on a roller coaster like this? Why or why not?

What did God say to the Israelites in Hosea about the roller coaster attitude they had toward Him?

What can keep you from having a roller coaster attitude with God?

PRAY ABOUT IT
- Thank God that His love for you is always steady and unchanging
- Ask God to help you not live a roller coaster life or have a roller coaster attitude with Him

WHAT ABOUT IT?
- With your family, dream about the perfect roller coaster. Talk about what it would be like—its features, twists, turns, spins, etc. You may even want to draw it out on a piece of paper
- Discuss how life can be like a roller coaster—with ups and downs, scary parts, thrilling parts, etc.
- Finish by explaining that the ride's creator always gets the passengers to the destination no matter how good or bad the coaster is. Similarly, God will get us to our

destination if we stay safely seated in His care

DAY 21

READ ABOUT IT: Matthew 11:28-30

Have you ever had an argument with a friend that went like this? "Hey, come here."

"Come here? No, you come over here," your friend replies.

"What? I asked you first. You come here!" You're getting a little annoyed now.

"I don't want to come over there. You have legs. Why don't you come here?!?" Your friend seems just as annoyed, and now neither of you wants to get near the other!

Those conversations are no fun! And they usually happen because of selfishness. Thankfully for us, God is *not* selfish. He was willing to come over to us first!

THINK ABOUT IT
Have you ever had an argument with someone similar to the one we just looked at?

How does Christmas prove that God is not selfish and was willing to come to us first?

After coming to us first, what does Jesus say in our Bible verses about coming to Him?

What are the benefits of coming to Jesus, according to our Bible verses?

Have you come to Jesus yet?

PRAY ABOUT IT
- Thank God for coming to you first
- Ask God to lead you closer and closer to Him

WHAT ABOUT IT?
- It is vital that you know the spiritual condition of each of your children
- Be sure to ask your children, even as young as four or five, if they have accepted Jesus as their Lord and Savior

DAY 22

READ ABOUT IT: 1 John 3:14-18

Have you ever seen the movie *The Little Mermaid*? If so, you may remember Arial singing a song called "Part of Your World." Listen to the lyrics:

Look at this stuff. Isn't it neat? Wouldn't you think my collection's complete? Wouldn't you think I'm the girl who has ev'rything? Look at this trove. Treasures untold, how many wonders can one cavern hold? Lookin' around here you'd think, sure she's got everything. I've got gadgets and gizmos aplenty. I've got whozits and whatzits galore. (You want thingamabobs? I got twenty.) But who cares? No big deal...I want more.

Unfortunately, at Christmas, we can be a lot like Arial. In spite of all that we have already, we want more presents and newer stuff. But when we spend all our time dreaming of more for ourselves, we miss out on how God would have us bless others.

THINK ABOUT IT
Would you say Arial's song was a selfish song or unselfish one?

How does focusing on yourself and what you want keep you from helping others get what they really need?

What do our Bible verses say about loving others?

How can you be a blessing to someone else this Christmas?

PRAY ABOUT IT
- Thank Jesus for giving up what He wanted, so that He could give us what we needed—forgiveness and eternal life
- Ask God to use you to bless others this Christmas

WHAT ABOUT IT?
- In case you are not familiar with the "Part of Your World" song, go to YouTube and type in the song title
- If your family is familiar with *The Little Mermaid*, you can discuss how Ariel's desire for more actually endangered the entire population of the sea

- She was so worried about what she wanted that she never considered how her choices might affect others
- Talk about how we can be a lot like Ariel, so focused on what we *want* for Christmas that we miss other people's *needs* this Christmas
- Discuss what your family can do to meet people's needs this holiday season

DAY 23

READ ABOUT IT: Luke 2:1-20

Fourteen year-old Matt was incredibly mad at his parents—so mad, in fact, that he refused to sleep in the same house as them! Instead, he chose to sleep in the attic. (Yes, that is still part of the same house, but don't tell Matt that!) Now, it was close to Christmas, in the middle of winter, and the attic roof was not insulated. That meant Matt spent the night in a freezing attic, sleeping on a rough piece of plywood. It was perhaps the worse night sleep he ever had in his whole life.

As we have talked about before, when it comes to the Christmas story, some people make it seem like the stable was a warm and cozy place. Yet, for Mary, Joseph, and Jesus, it was far colder and much less comfortable than Matt's attic!

THINK ABOUT IT
What was the worst night sleep you have ever gotten?

What do you think it was like for Mary and Joseph in that stable?

Why do you think that God was willing to be born in such a place as that?

What can you do for God because of all that He has done for you?

PRAY ABOUT IT
- Thank God for all that He has done for you
- Ask God to use you to praise Him, bless others, and make a mighty difference in the world

WHAT ABOUT IT?
- On Day 13, it was suggested that you set up dominos (or use *Lego* pieces, *Scrabble* tiles, or hard cover books). Do so again, setting up ten to twelve in a row
- Gather the family around what you have set up and talk about how Jesus came to a messed up earth as a baby, being born in a cold and dirty stable. He did that because He planned to bless us in so many awesome ways
- Now that we have been blessed, it is our job to turn around and bless others
- Knock over the first domino and watch them all fall down

- Go on to discuss how Jesus blesses us, so we can turn around and bless others. Those people that we blessed, start to bless others...and it just keeps going
- Set up the dominos again. This time leave one out, creating a space for a domino in the middle to fall without striking another
- Talk about how when someone steps out of the cycle by not blessing others, the cycle stops and the next person doesn't get blessed
- Commit as a family to always be part of the cycle

DAY 24

READ ABOUT IT: Matthew 2:1-12

As soon as Ryan became a teenager, he started having doubts about God. "Is He real? How can I know? Is everything my parents and my pastor say about Him true?" Ryan was really struggling with this.

One particularly bad day, when everything seemed to be going wrong, Ryan just shouted out to his dad, "I don't believe in God anymore!"

Surprisingly, Ryan's dad did not get upset or even seem shocked. He just pulled his son close, looked him in the eye, and said, "That's okay, son. He still believes in you."

THINK ABOUT IT
Do you ever have doubts about God? If so, what are they?

How does the Christmas story show that God still believes in us, even when we don't believe in Him?

Why is Christmas the most important time of the year?

How will you celebrate what God has done for you this Christmas?

PRAY ABOUT IT
- Thank God for how much He loves and believes in you
- Ask God to strengthen your trust in Him

WHAT ABOUT IT?
- Ask your children if they have any doubts about God
- If so, discuss them and talk them through
- Be sure to go to a Christmas Eve service at a Bible believing church
- On Day 1, we talked about having a birthday cake ready for Jesus on Christmas day. Do you have one ready?

DAY 25

READ ABOUT IT: 1 Peter 4:8-10

The good news: Christmas is here!

The bad news: When this day is over, Christmas won't be back for a whole year!

Maybe you've spent today playing with, or using, the gift you've really been hoping for. Or maybe you are a little disappointed because you really didn't get what you wanted.

But whether you are happy or sad with what you got, think about this. Is Jesus happy with what *you* are giving Him? After all, it is Jesus' birthday, not yours.

Now, you might be thinking, "What in the world can I give to Jesus!?!? He's God! What does He need?"

Well, Jesus has given you *lots* of things (like money, clothes, toys, talents, abilities, and experiences), and in return He wants you to use them to glorify Him and bless others—not keep them for yourself.

THINK ABOUT IT
What has God made you really good at?

What gifts do we have from God according to our Bible verses for today?

What are you doing with the gifts God has given you?

Who can you bless this Christmas season?

PRAY ABOUT IT
- Thank God for all the many things that He has given you
- Ask God to show you how you can use those things to glorify Him and to bless others

WHAT ABOUT IT?
- Get out the birthday cake for Jesus and sing happy birthday to Him
- Give everyone a piece of cake and talk about what it means to glorify God
- The word "glorify" in the New Testament literally means "brightness." That means that our lives and actions should *shine out*, so people can see all the greatness of God
- To better illustrate this, get out a flashlight and mirror

- Point the mirror toward yourself and shine the flashlight at it. The light will reflect off and shine back on you. Discuss how when we use our gifts and talents for ourselves, no one gets to experience God's glory because it is all about us
- Turn the mirror around and shine the flashlight at it again, angle the mirror so that it hits each family member one at a time
- Discuss how when we use our gifts and talents to help others, then people can see God's glory and be blessed by it

DAY 26

READ ABOUT IT: John 6:1-15

Way back in 1884, there was a little girl named Hattie May. One Sunday she stood near a small church crying. "There's no room for me in Sunday School," she sobbed as Pastor Conwell walked by. Taking her by the hand, the kind pastor found a place for her in a class. The child was so touched that she went to bed that night determined to help children who had no place to worship Jesus. Two years later, Hattie died, and her parents called for the kind hearted Pastor Conwell to handle the final arrangements.

As Hattie's little body was being moved, a worn and crumpled purse was found. Inside sat 57 cents and a note which read, "This is to help build the little church bigger so more children can go to Sunday school." Inspired by the devotion of this little girl from a very poor family, the pastor challenged his deacons to get busy and raise enough money for a larger building. In a short while, Hattie May's 57 cents had increased to $250; a large sum for 1886! Her unselfish love had impacted hundreds of people! Today, what Hattie May started is now Temple University and Temple University Hospital!

THINK ABOUT IT
What did Hattie May give, and what did Jesus turn it into?

What did the little boy in our Bible story give, and what did Jesus turn it into?

You may not think that you have much to offer Jesus. But what can you give, so Jesus can turn it into something great?

PRAY ABOUT IT
- Thank God because He can take little things and make them big!
- Ask God to take what you offer Him and use it to do great and awesome things

WHAT ABOUT IT?
- Talk with your family about some God-honoring gift you can all save for in 2018
- Some ideas to help you start brainstorming can be found on the Samaritan's Purse website under "Gift Catalogue"
- Get some poster board and create a "fundraising chart." Draw a large thermometer or ruler and use that to chart

your progress until you reach your designated goal

DAY 27

READ ABOUT IT: 2 Corinthians 9:6-9

Thirteen year-old Teddy just celebrated his birthday. He didn't always like having his birthday and Christmas so close together. But one good thing about it was that he got a *whole lot* of money. It wasn't often that Teddy had a bunch of cash in his wallet, so it was an exciting time for him.

Sitting in church as the offering plate came around, the new teenager opened his wallet. He had six twenty dollar bills and one dollar bill. Now Teddy didn't want to just give the one, but he sure didn't want to give a twenty either! He quickly thought about putting in a twenty and asking for change from the usher, but that would have been embarrassing. So, he just put in the one.

THINK ABOUT IT
When it comes to putting money in the offering or making donations to Christian charities, are you generous?

Our Bible verses say that God wants us to be "cheerful givers." When you give, do you give cheerfully?

What do our Bible verses say happens when we give?

If you haven't always been the best, or most cheerful, giver, what can help you do better in this coming year?

PRAY ABOUT IT
- Thank God that He gave His one and only Son. It was indeed the best thing He could give!
- Ask God to give you a generous spirit and a desire to share what He has blessed you with

WHAT ABOUT IT?
- Give each of your kids two quarters and have them place one in each hand, then tightly form a fist around the quarters
- Take out a five dollar bill and tell your kids that you want to bless them with five dollars. Attempt to place it in their hands…which is impossible when they are "tight-fisted"

- Discuss how God also wants to bless us with things, but He cannot when we are tightly holding on to other things
- We need to release what God has blessed us with, so He can bless us with more things
- The cycle keeps going until we close our hands and don't release what we already have to make room for more

DAY 28

READ ABOUT IT: Matthew 6:19-21; 6:33

The day after Thanksgiving has come to be known as "Black Friday." It is a day when mobs of people go out shopping for the best bargains. Funny how the day after we thank God for all He has given us, we rush out to get more stuff!

During Black Friday, people will stand in lines for hours—even at 3:00 a.m.—waiting to get into a store so they can buy something on sale. Sometimes, people want these deals so badly that they do not-so-nice things. One year, a woman peppered sprayed people away from a discounted TV she wanted. And at another store, when there were only a few X-boxes left, dozens of shoppers attacked and fought each other to get one.

THINK ABOUT IT
Do you want something bad enough to stand in line for hours at 3:00 a.m.?

What does Jesus have to say about things and possessions in verses 19-21?

What does Jesus say should be our focus in verse 33?

What will be your focus in 2018?

PRAY ABOUT IT
- Thank God for His great love and care for you. Thank Him also for the truth of His Word
- Ask God to help you focus on building up His kingdom, not building up a pile of possessions

WHAT ABOUT IT?
- Tell the family you are all going to play a game of charades
- Select someone to be the first person to try to act out a word of your choosing
- While this person is attempting to act it out, block the view of the others as best you can
- When they start to complain, talk about how, when something is blocking our view, we have trouble focusing on other things
- Likewise, when we are focused on what we want and what we like, that ends up blocking our view of all the things God wants us to do for others

- After you make this point, go ahead and play charades the right way

DAY 29

READ ABOUT IT: Mark 16:15

Imagine walking with a friend on a wooded path. You notice a poisonous rattlesnake at the edge of the underbrush. Instead of warning your friend, you simply move to the other side of the path. While your friend is watching you move to the other side of the path and wondering what in the world you are doing, the snake strikes! It jabs sharp fangs into your friend's calf and injects burning venom.

Your friend screams in pain and runs for it. After several yards, the friend collapses. "Why didn't you tell me there was a rattlesnake!?!"

Meanwhile, you are wondering what all the screaming is about. "Hey, I got you a Christmas present this year. *And*, I moved to the other side of the path to be a good example for you. What else do you want!?!?"

THINK ABOUT IT
Do you think, if this story were true, that you would be a good friend to this person?

Sometimes, we think if we do nice things for people and be a good example, then that is good enough. But why wasn't getting a Christmas present and moving to the other side of the path good enough for your friend in this story?

Jesus doesn't just want us doing nice things for people and acting nice in front of them. That alone won't save people from their sins. What does Jesus say we must do?

Who can you tell about Jesus in 2018?

PRAY ABOUT IT
- Thank Jesus for coming to give you a new life
- Ask God to use you to tell others about Him in 2018, so they can be saved from the poisonous effects of sin

WHAT ABOUT IT?
- Create a list of three to five friends, relatives, associates, neighbors, and/or classmates that you know need Jesus as their Lord and Savior

- Place that list in a prayer basket that should become the centerpiece on your kitchen table
- Be sure to pray for the people on that list every night before dinner in 2018

DAY 30

READ ABOUT IT: Ephesians 5:15-17

During his church's Live Nativity, seven year-old Jacob got to be a shepherd for the first time with his dad. For the part, he and his dad had to walk over to the stable to greet Mary, Joseph, and baby Jesus. Then they stood and waited for the wise men to show up. For *every one* of the performances, when the wise men started moving toward the stable, Jacob would lean toward his dad and whisper, "Here come the wise guys!"

Well, you are on the verge of a whole new year. 2017 is just about gone, and 2018 is just about here. And, in 2018, you can choose to be a wise man (or woman) or a wise guy. There is a big difference between the two you know!

THINK ABOUT IT
What do you think is the difference between a wise person and wise guy?

What do our Bible verses say we should do?

How will you discover what the Lord wants you to do in 2018?

PRAY ABOUT IT
- Thank God for 2017
- Ask God to help you live wisely in 2018

WHAT ABOUT IT?
- Make a list of goals for 2018. Each family member should have at least five
- Have an educational goal (like study each day), a family goal (like be nicer to my sister), a spiritual goal (like pray 15 minutes each day), a life goal (like read ten books this year), and a personal goal (like do something nice for a neighbor)
- Place these lists on the refrigerator or some other prominent place where they will be seen often
- Don't stop doing devotions as a family. Grab another of my 30 Day Devotional books!

EPILOGUE

I hope God has truly blessed your family during this 30-Day journey. I know He deeply desires to do so many awesome things in and through you. His plan for your family is truly remarkable! I trust you have grabbed hold of that.

If you have been blessed in any way through these 30-Days, please do me the great favor of leaving a positive review on Amazon. Your review just may encourage another family to take this same journey.

Be sure to check other devotionals in the TABLE TALKS series!

GOD BLESS YOU!

Made in the USA
Monee, IL
11 November 2019